Praise for Hot Silver

"For me, the best travel writing makes me think not *I wish I had done that*, but *I'm so glad I didn't! Hot Silver* — a reminder that sometimes our travel daydreams are as good as it gets — had me laughing, commiserating and vowing *never* to do what Lewis did: travel across Australia by train. I'm glad he did it though, because it's produced an unique and entertaining tale. Highly recommended."
- Catherine Ryan Howard, author of *Backpacked* and *Mousetrapped*

"I knew I was in for a treat the moment I got to the end of the introduction to Steven Lewis' *Hot Silver - Riding the Indian Pacific*. It not so much took off as galloped. A master of irony, Steven Lewis' razor sharp wit is delivered with deadpan accuracy. I found myself chortling with laughter throughout, unable to put it down until the glorious end."
— Victoria Ugarte, "Postcards from Millie"

"A vivid and highly entertaining insight into the beauty and eccentricities of a rail journey across the Australian landscape."
- Geoff Bartlett, travel writer and author

Hot
SILVER

Riding the Indian Pacific

Also by Steven Lewis

How to Format Perfect Kindle Books
In-Book Promotion: Kindle Features to Increase Sales
Kindle for Newspapers, Magazines and Blogs
Kindle Automation for Mac
The Rocks Self-Guided Walking Tour
Sydney Opera House & Botanic Gardens
– A Self-Guided Walk

Hot SILVER

Riding the Indian Pacific

STEVEN LEWIS

Taleist
Sydney, 2011

Hot Silver — Riding the Indian Pacific
by
Steven Lewis
Copyright © 2011 Taleist
Published 2011 by Taleist
No part of this book may be used or reproduced in any manner without written permission.
All trademarks used in the book are the property of their respective owners.
Cover by Design for Writers
www.designforwriters.com
All rights reserved.

ISBN-13: 978-0-9808559-5-1
ISBN-10: 0-9808559-5-0

For Fleur,
who left me in Adelaide
but supported me all the way

*But the true voyagers are only those who leave
Just to be leaving; hearts light, like balloons,
They never turn aside from their fatality
And without knowing why they always say: "Let's go!"*
— Baudelaire, *The Voyage*

The world's great powers have long declared themselves through their rail lines.
                                         Simon Winchester
                                         Vanity Fair, October 2011

In May 2010 my wife, Fleur, and I were given first class passage from Sydney to Perth on the Indian Pacific. The trip was provided by Great Southern Rail because we were making an audio travel feature for an Australian airline.
The journey across Australia by train was one I'd always wanted to take. In fact Fleur had been thinking about surprising me for my fortieth birthday the following year with a trip on either the Indian Pacific or the Ghan, both operated by GSR.

Less often than you would think do travel writers get to relax and actually take the holidays they write about. Unless you're AA Gill or Paul Theroux, you simply can't make enough money writing about lying on a beach or riding a train to pay for time spent lying on a beach or riding a train. Lonely Planet writers seem to have an enviable job but it's one that involves racing around sticking their heads into as many guest houses, hotels, cafés and roadside stalls as they can in the least possible time and with their expenses scrutinised by bean counters at home. All the time they're scribbling away, hoping they've got enough detail, and praying they don't lose their notes or get something wrong. There's always a reader who'll be quick to email the editor if they have.

Chances are that you'll read only one piece on a place by a particular travel writer. It's most likely, however, that he's turned one trip into five, six or ten pieces with different angles for several publications. Dubai's souks for one newspaper, its luxury hotels for another paper's colour supplement, four-wheel driving in the desert for a men's mag, and so on. All the time he's competing with every would-be travel writer with a blog and a digital SLR. The cost of entry to the travel writing business is low but it's hard work and you'll want a holiday afterwards.

That's why I don't do that anymore. My wife and I decided that our travel features would be only about places we wanted to go and where we were willing to take the time and make a holiday of it. We've had some fantastic experiences as a result.

I'm just not sure the Indian Pacific was one of them.

Steven Lewis
Sydney
2011

Day One
ALL ABOARD

· Sydney ·

The fleeces gave me the first twinge of concern. Fleeces are worn for work by mechanics, hardware stores clerks and zookeepers. You won't be checked in by a receptionist in a fleece at the Four Seasons, even if it's at the North Pole. And my expectation of the Indian Pacific was that it was essentially a Four Seasons lowered onto its side and rolled from ocean to ocean on velvet tracks. In my mind great train journeys should be like the golden days of the Raj played out on rails.

So yes, it jars me that the doughy attendant at the door of our Gold Class carriage is wearing a company fleece. I later find out that Great Southern Rail calls these frontline staff "hospitality assistants", "HAs" for short. This hospitality assistant is wearing the sort of shoes particular to distinct branches of the hospitality industry. I'm thinking of the branches where the guests are there involuntarily: hospitals, prisons and — I'm getting ahead of myself here — old people's homes. In these corners of the hospitality game you're less likely to be assisted to a glass of Champagne than to the toilet or back to your cell.

Fleur had seen this coming. She never believed this was going to be a luxurious trip. She'd hedged her bets by agreeing to come but only as far as Adelaide. From there she had booked a flight home. This meant she would not be joining me for the long, hot passage across the Nullarbor to Perth. More fool her, I thought, and reinforced my cleverness by not saying that out loud.

Looking back at the pictures we took on the platform at Sydney's Country Rail terminal, I see now for the first time that Fleur actually looks frightened. I took the picture of us by holding the camera at arm's length. The train is behind us and Fleur is looking wide-eyed into the lens, like a hostage. This is not the face of a woman who expects to be spending the next day and a half in a luxurious incubator.

It's the face of a woman dragged by her kids to the amusement park and about to get on a ride she suspects is maintained by spliff-smoking teens handpicked for their records of negligence and absenteeism.

I see that now but I couldn't see it from where I was then, by her side grinning into the camera like a loon.

Not for the first time in our relationship I had ignored her good sense in favour of what I wished to be true. I wished for the Indian Pacific to take me back in time as much as across the country. I wished to travel like Poirot in a lavish TV adaptation of *Murder on the Orient Express*, all white gloves, whistles and explosions of steam. I wished to believe that the smart casual dress code for dinner specified on GSR's website was a reluctant concession by the Dining Standards Committee to the fact that so few of us own black tie these days.

My enthusiasm for the trip in the weeks leading up to it swelled in inverse proportion to Fleur's apprehension. To jolly her along I became almost rabidly excited; she wondered about chaining herself to our front gate.

Things had got off to a great start as far as I was concerned. My father-in-law had driven us on a short, traffic-free journey to Sydney's Central Station in a German car that holds out your seatbelt for you after you sit down. If a two-door car could provide that sort of service mechanically, imagine what could be done by a 23-carriage train with a full staff.

The Country Link terminal of Central Station turns out to be exactly what I need to keep the fantasy stoked. From the outside Walter Liberty Vernon's classical sandstone building is imposing but not ostentatious. Inside it's cool and stately. Natural light floods the Grand Concourse from the glass strip running along the centre of a vaulted roof supported on steel. Like much of Sydney's colonial architecture, the terminal feels like a dollhouse rendering of a memory from another place. This section of

HOT SILVER

Australia's largest railway station housed the original steam platforms and it does recall the great Steam Age stations of London but in miniature.

The terminal is just the sort of place where a journey like this should start. The building is as solid as the trains that pull in here but infused with the possibilities that come with long-distance travel.

In the time since the invention of the railway we've launched men and monkeys into space. I don't care. It's still fantastic to me that there's a place across the road from an actors' college and a couple of backpackers' hostels where I can step from a platform onto a machine that will hardly stop until it's on the other side of Australia.

It's in this impressionable state of mind that I encounter FP1, a railcar with an Art Deco body the shape of a minibus. She was built to run along rail tracks on four wheels, carrying small groups of passengers on branch lines where a whole train was unnecessary.

FP1 was exhibited on the Grand Concourse to showcase her successful restoration by railway apprentices, and they had certainly done the old girl proud. Under the light flooding through the glass ceiling, she gleamed in a two-tone enamel coat of light green and cream paint. Her interior, visible through her wide-windows, was immaculate and inviting.

Up to 18 passengers would have sat mostly in two-seater benches facing forward. The driver sat among the passengers on a cushioned chair upholstered in green vinyl. At his left hand the brake handle rose up from the floor; to his right sat a few large dials embedded in a dashboard under the window. He wasn't separated from the passengers in a driver's cabin, he was among them. FP1 was like an inviting Kombi van on rails.

In short, I wanted one.

In my mind's eye I saw her filled with jolly bands of travellers riding the rails with the driver in the middle as host. I could see the men on their way to work in fedoras and skinny ties, newspapers heavy with the dark clouds forming over 1930s Europe. The men would smile and nod a greeting when a familiar travelling companion came aboard. Sometimes they would cause the girls in cloche hats to blush at a flirtation. So convivial is the journey that later some of the fedoras and cloche hats will marry.

I'm so excited about my own romantic journey across Australia, it's possible I'm developing a fever.

A little post-trip research tells me my reaction to the friendly rail bus is consistent with my other fantasies about Australian rolling stock. That is to say it's entirely out of kilter with the majority. Introduced in 1937, the rail buses were unpopular and withdrawn only two years later. Had I known this, I might have been wary of falling in love again moments later. There on Platform 2 was a mighty silver tube running for hundreds of metres, each carriage smartly badged in burnt orange with the Indian Pacific name under a silhouette of its emblem, the wedge-tailed eagle.

And there on Platform 3 was the same thing. The Indian Pacific is so long that it needs two platforms. When it's time to go the locomotive must pull the cars on Platform 3 forward then reverse so they can be coupled to the cars on Platform 2. The result is more than half a kilometre of hot silver that will snake its way across the continent over the next 65 hours.

After our tickets are checked by the befleeced attendant at the carriage door we're allowed onto the train to make our way down the narrow corridor to our double compartment. There are no other identity checks or security screenings, one of the lingering civilities of train travel.

The door of our compartment is marked by an Art Deco light fixture illuminating "11" and "12", the numbers of our berths. The thin compartment is clad in the same light wood veneer as the corridor. A three-seater bench runs from the door to a picture window. The bench is upholstered in a hard-wearing mauve and green fabric

HOT SILVER

more in keeping with a budget airline than my Orient Express fantasies.

There's a reasonable amount of leg room between the bench and the wall of the compartment. There's a power socket, a shallow cupboard for our jackets and an ample shelf for our bags. Because this is Gold Class, the premium class on the Indian Pacific, a door in the wall is for the en suite bathroom, a feature the Great Southern Rail website had referenced but not described. I can see why. If there had been room for a bathroom on Apollo 11, it might have looked like this; and the astronauts might still have preferred to pee down their legs.

It's a grim, dimly-lit space, a pale green box rendered in an easy-wipe Formica. Mounted in the wall is a stainless steel sink stowed like an airplane tray table. When you want it, you pull the latch and lower it with a metallic clank. Lifting it back into place slowly is what sends the contents gurgling into the bowels of the train. Or onto the tracks. I don't know. What I do know is the toilet works the same way — a bedpan that also folds out of the wall. It's under the sink so you can't have them both out at the same time, unless you're a midget contortionist. It makes going to the toilet a sequence of clicks and clanks.

Clunk click before each shit.

The bathroom includes a shower nozzle in one corner of the ceiling. There is a shower curtain but what for, I don't know, because we will find out later that everything in the room gets soaked whatever you do. Afterwards, there's a towel about a foot square to dry off on. At the Four Seasons the toilet paper would be more absorbent.

The working of the toilet and other features is explained to us during our departure safety briefing, which happens individually in each compartment. Our friendly hospitality assistant takes us through the safety features. I can't remember what they were. What could they be? In the event of a train crash, I imagine the exits are fairly obvious, if you're alive. There will probably even be some new ones. It's really a question of whether you're unmangled enough to get to them. I'm pretty sure there weren't any slides or life rafts.

The steward also asked us whether we would like the early or the later meal sitting. Once you have been issued with a red or a blue ticket, you are locked into that sitting for the duration of the trip. There are two dining cars on our train but too many Gold Class passengers for a single sitting.

Aside from there being no life jacket demonstration and having to have the toilet explained to you, the only real difference between our in-compartment safety briefing and the safety briefing on a plane is that we're issued with a maintenance card. If we notice anything in the compartment that needs fixing, we're to jot it down on the card. This seems suspiciously like someone's job, not something for passengers to do. What would Poirot have said if handed a maintenance card on the Orient Express? "For you, 'Astings."

Also incongruous with the luxury price tag of the trip is the fact that the razor sharp single-ply toilet paper is in a locked dispenser. Passengers have paid thousands for a two-and-a-half day trip across the country in Gold Class, one that includes three-course meals thrice daily. Are the same people going to be stuffing their luggage with cheap loo roll? Other than to teach my arse some kind of lesson, I can't see any reason to use more than the least possible amount of this loo paper. I suppose I could have been tempted to rip off a few sheets to start on some of the jobs on my maintenance card.

When the steward moves on to conscript the next compartment to the maintenance staff, we're left to settle in. We decide to leave our compartment door open like the friendly people we're not. Our fellow passengers fall into two categories, those who walk past and don't look in and those who pass with heads at full swivel. Occasionally a woman in a cook's jacket bustles past, the keys on her belt jangling. The sound of great bunches of keys passing outside our compartment becomes one of the signature

HOT SILVER

sounds of the Indian Pacific. Perhaps drawing lessons from the murder on the Orient Express, it seems much is under lock and key on this train.

The train departs on time at 2.55 in the afternoon. I'm excited, Fleur looks resigned. I take public transport infrequently so even the Sydney city views from the train are fresh to me. It's amazing how quickly the view changes. In just over an hour we go from city centre office blocks to inner city railway terraces and then the eucalypt forests whose coloured haze gives the Blue Mountains their name.

Influenced by Paul Theroux, as any travel writer on a train must be, I'd had visions of reading volumes aboard the train. In my excitement I'm torn between pulling out one of the tomes I've brought with me and looking out the window. So much to do!

At 4 p.m. Fleur and I make our first attempt on the lounge car to get a drink. It doesn't go well. Pushing through the heavy door into the bar car causes the needle to jump from the metaphorical record player. It's a Western where the hero walks into the saloon and the piano player stops playing. A silence didn't exactly descend but there was a definite stiffening in seats and an air of, "And where do *you* think *you're* going to sit?" The car has a selection of seats, benches running under the windows and a single table for two. All are taken.

My naivety about train travel was becoming clearer by the minute. It hadn't occurred to me that there wouldn't be enough seats in the bar car for the number of passengers to whom its hospitality had been promised. This, however, wasn't my biggest mistake. My biggest mistake was that we were early for drinks, at least 30 years too early. Looking around the bar, the average age was over 70. The next year I would be 40 and the parent of a teenager so I hadn't been feeling like a spring chicken for a while. In this crowd, however, Fleur and I are adolescents.

The response we are getting was the same reaction our fellow passengers would have got emerging through the fog of youthful pheromones onto a Contiki bus. Close quarters travel doesn't tolerate great differences, we are clearly very different and we aren't being tolerated.

We retreat.

An hour later we are thirsty enough to mount a second attack on the bar car. This time the table for two is free. John Denver and the Carpenters are taking turns on the stereo. At the bar there's a slow-moving queue to book tickets for tours of Broken Hill and Adelaide.

Stubbies of Crown and VB have loosened tongues and the mood is convivial. They're making friends and we're now being tolerated, or at least ignored. Behind us a grey-haired American is telling his new chums he's not rich but he lives off investment properties in California. He and his wife — she's just down there talking to John — saw a TV program about train journeys in Australia so here they are. A septuagenarian in a collared sports shirt is propping up the bar. A set of clip-on braces secures the waist band of his jeans an inch south of his nipples. Monte Carlo this is not.

There are lots of good natured getting-to-know-you jokes. Tonight they hope the driver is on the right road; and tomorrow they'll hope he has GPS. The day after, every bump will lead to a joke about potholes on the roads.

Buoyed by a bit more success, we decide to return to our compartment to dress for dinner. When Fleur wants to pull down the blind to get changed, I point at the ink-black night over the deserted Blue Mountains. "Who the hell is going to see you?" I ask. Fleur doesn't need to reply because at exactly that moment the compartment is flooded with bright light. We have pulled into Lithgow train station, its platform packed with people curious to look into the windows of the famous Indian Pacific. Fleur says nothing as she pulls down the blind and gets changed.

HOT SILVER

It transpires that my wife almost become a Lithgow legend for nothing. Aboard the Indian Pacific "smart casual" is interpreted as "anything goes", right down to tracksuit trousers for men who look like they haven't jogged anywhere since the Battle of the Somme. The ladies favour vibrant floral prints or fleeces in various shades of purple, suggesting a lucrative gap in the womenswear market for floral fleeces. Sneakers are the footwear of choice for men and women alike.

We reach the Queen Adelaide dining car by walking through the bar car, past a glass display case of souvenir windcheaters and stubby holders. The adjacent magazine rack is stuffed with free copies of *Take 5* and *That's Life*, women's magazines for the blue-rinse set.

The restaurant car is elegant. Etched glass panels separate dark-wood booths laid with heavy white cloths and cutlery for three courses. Backlit coving stencilled with "AR" in regal script runs the length of the carriage. Here for the first time is the glamour I've been craving. Except there's one hitch. The booths are for four. I realise with horror that each meal will be taken with two strangers. We'd managed to curdle the bar car just by entering it; now two people are going to have to sit *with* us.

This time that lucky couple were Heather and her husband, Bede, retirees from Queensland.

Bede is well into his seventies. Heather, who might be younger, is in a figure-hugging red turtle neck with round clear-framed glasses that take up much of her face. She has the sort of teeth that keep Americans from travelling, especially when they're stained by bar car red wine. Bede is in a blue-check flannel shirt with a V-neck jumper. He has the face of a man who doesn't put up with any nonsense and who has a broad definition of nonsense.

The menu offers choices for each course. There's a wine list but, unlike the food, wine isn't included with Gold Class passage and hardly anyone orders wine or beer. For those who order wine, the staff will hang onto the bottles between meals. That way a bottle can last the whole trip.

The food is impressive. We start with a choice between Middle Eastern lentil soup and a grilled baguette with prawns. It's chicken breast, tenderloin or Tasmanian salmon for mains. And dessert brings a choice between the Outback Cheese Plate or cheese in cake-form.

We make much of how amazing it is that such a delicious meal should come from a narrow galley on a moving train. It *is* truly incredible the topic is also a life preserver keeping us from drowning in awkward silence. The booths are too cramped to talk separately to one's companion so it's all for chat or chat for none. Heather talks gamely about their small village in Queensland. Bede chews hard, making no secret of the fact that he'd have voted for silence. We try our best, asking questions, listening hard, and searching for topics of interest to Heather and Bede. I don't know whether we could have done better or if we never had a chance. Bede gives the impression that he'd rather give a ferret the run of his trousers than face dinner-length conversation with us. I know how he feels but I work to hide it. If Bede has ever been susceptible to similar social pressures, he's chewing through it tonight.

After dinner there is a reception in the bar car for our dinner sitting. The other sitting has already had the reception and is now at dinner. The configuration of the train varies depending on demand. Judy, one of the hospitality assistants, gives us some facts and figures about our train. Tonight we're in one of 23 carriages, making up 630 metres of train.

Around us everyone is having a wonderful time, staff and travellers. There are more jokes about the driver being on the right road; and we find out that daughter of Dean, the train's night manager, has joined the Indian Pacific family and is making her first trip today. She waves from behind the bar.

When we return to our compartment the top bunk has

been folded down and the beds made up. White sheets give the compartment a touch of the elegance of the dining car. A chocolate in a black Indian Pacific wrapper on each pillow is a welcome touch, although it reminds me of the After Eights my parents used to hand out at dinner parties.

Brushing our teeth in the bedpan sink takes some of the gloss off the apple but I am excited nonetheless. Heather had told us that sleeping on a train is like being rocked to sleep. This had created an unwelcome mental image of Bede tucked up in his bunk but I was looking forward to a good sleep.

The last time I'd slept on a train was a six-week school trip overland from Kowloon Station in Hong Kong to Liverpool Street in London. I didn't remember having any trouble sleeping on the trains but I'd been 17 and exhausted by days of tours and talking crap. Also at least some of the nights I'd been drunk on "screwdrivers" we mixed with Tang and rocket fuel from a foreign currency store in Ulan Bator.

Fleur takes the top bunk, which I think is brave — it doesn't have a safety rail. It was better for me to have the bottom one because — at what I am no longer thinking of as my advanced age — I am more likely to need to clunk click in the night. I wouldn't trust myself spelunking down the tiny ladder in the dark.

Sleeping on the train turns out to be nothing like being rocked to sleep. It's more like being poked randomly by a malevolent force that senses when you're about to drop off and pokes just a bit harder. I start to drift off then snap back when the train rattles round a corner or pulls into a station. As soon as I get used to being stationary we lurch off again. Lying in the narrow bunk I fixate on how hot and airless it is in the compartment, something about which we can do nothing. There's no individual control in the Gold Class compartments and the windows don't open. The website had advised warm clothes for the evenings "as the air-conditioning can be cool". Cool like dragon's breath. It feels like the communal thermostat has been set by a committee of old people who argued between hot and hotter before compromising on hottest. Normally when I'm up and down all night it's not because I'm trying to get fluid *into* me.

I must have drifted off for at least a while because I wake up to see Fleur perched like a spectre at the end of my bunk with a glass of water in her hand. Is it recrimination I see in her eyes?

The Grand Concourse, Central Station, Sydney

Us

STEVEN LEWIS

Them

Home for three days

HOT SILVER

Fleur curdling the bar car

Queen Adelaide dining car

Clunk click

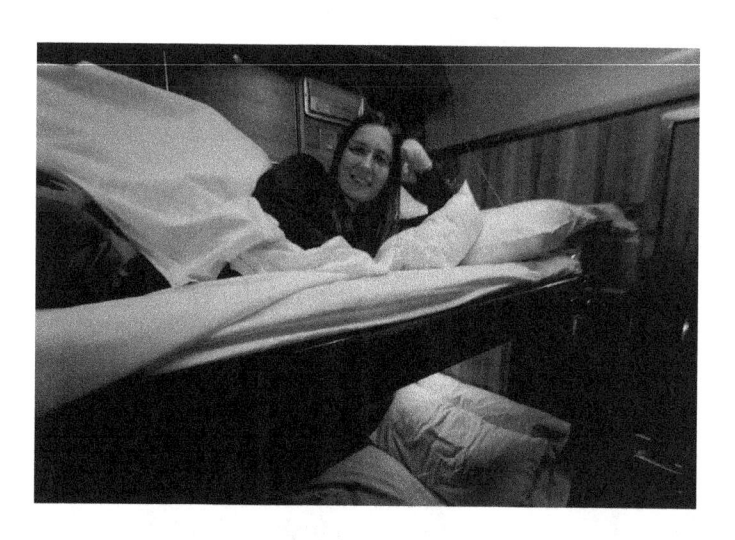

Ready to rock

· The Train ·

The Indian Pacific first rolled across Australia in 1970, named for the two oceans it connected. Despite the name, that first train travelled Pacific to Indian, just as we were doing in its fortieth anniversary year. The continuing importance of the route in connecting the country to the ocean capitals of Sydney, Adelaide and Perth is reflected in the itemised tariff for stowed baggage. For the benefit of the younger "Red Class" passengers, it's dominated by items like Eskys, surfboards, boogie boards and surf skis. I certainly can't imagine Bede has stashed a boogie board in the baggage car.

Sydney's Central Station is only a few kilometres from the birthplace of European Australia at Sydney Cove. From there the Indian Pacific proceeds inland, slowly at first because of the steep curves in the track over the Blue Mountains. It will also stop from time to time to give way to freight trains. It's freight that pays the way on Australia's railways so passengers must be sidelined for goods, even if they're paying $2,100 per person for a Gold Class sleeper.

Once over the mountains the train travels west towards the halfway mark, the South Australian capital of Adelaide. There it stops for a few hours before heading north to Port Augusta. After that it cuts pretty much a straight line across the top of the Great Australian Bight, through the dry and mostly uninhabited bottom of the continent.

The whole journey is 4,352 kilometres, which is roughly the width of the continental United States.

For passengers like us there are whistle stops of a few hours in the mining town of Broken Hill, New South Wales; Adelaide; and Kalgoorlie, another mining town in Western Australia. We pass through other notable spots like Mt Canobolas, just southwest of Orange, which at

1,395 metres is the highest point of land between Sydney and Perth. We also go through Parkes, home of the radio telescope used to receive live images of the Apollo 11 moon landing in 1969 and transmit them to the States. This part of its history was memorialised in the Sam Neill film *The Dish*. The Parkes Observatory is still a world force in astronomy, responsible for the discovery of half the known pulsars in the universe. It could be discovering a pulsar at the exact moment we pass closest to it on this trip. The fact is that it doesn't really matter what you're passing close to if you're not going to stop or even see it from the window.

This is something I discover in my research for this trip. Most of the books I can find are filled with information about things the train passes over or close to but that passengers won't get to experience anymore than air travellers experience the places they fly over. There are amazing views from the train and the chance to see wonderful scenery but what's 20 kilometres over that hill doesn't seem to me to have anything to do with the trip.

Day Two
MUFFINS AT DAWN

· Broken Hill ·

The final bell on the first night's fight for sleep is rung by the PA system announcing our imminent arrival in Broken Hill 10 minutes before sunrise. We throw ourselves out of bed and each take a turn in the shower to wake up and cool off. Not only am I exhausted but the dry heat overnight has slashed at my throat like a razor; and my nose is running faster than Usain Bolt and in a similar shade of green. I stuff a handful of toilet paper in my jacket and, yes, if it weren't locked up, I would have taken more. Score one, Great Southern Rail cost cutters.

The PA told us that there were muffins in the bar car for those who wanted a snack before heading off on the bus tour of Broken Hill. It didn't warn us that what our travelling companions lacked in youth they made up for in early-rising and cunning. By the time we get to the bar car not five minutes later there's nothing left but crumbs and a queue of fleeces heading the other way with bulging handbags. We make our way onto the platform bested, hungry and with a new regard for our companions.

I am half asleep with a throat that feels like someone scraped it hard with a loo brush but I would have to have been dead not to appreciate the view on the platform. The Indian Pacific, still silver and still magnificent, stands under a dawn sky that's just starting to turn blue. Streaks of cloud cut across it in golds, reds and pinks like brush strokes in an oil painting. It's a stunning sight on a crisp morning. We are further into Australia than I've ever been and I feel privileged to be seeing such an iconic part of it.

Across from the platform two smart coaches are waiting, the sort where passengers sit high above the action like a theatre audience.

Broken Hill is in New South Wales but on the border with South Australia and Adelaide is closer than Sydney.

Nicknamed Silver City, its business since it was founded in 1883 has been extracting the good stuff from one of the world's largest silver-lead-zinc mineral deposits. Its dependence on mining is written on every street. Literally. The Post Office sits on the corner of Chloride and Argent streets. Further into town Radium Street runs parallel to Uranium Street and so it goes on. The map of Broken Hill is an urban periodic table.

Seen in a satellite photograph Broken Hill has giant open wounds where other cities might have parks. The broken hill that gave the town its name was long ago peeled to the ground then turned into a hole by miners extracting its 1,800 million-year-old core.

The Broken Hill Proprietary Company that was born in the city became Australia's largest mining company. BHP's merger with Billiton in 2001 took it to another level, becoming part of not just Australia's largest miner but the world's biggest mining company. By market capitalisation BHP Billiton is one of the world's largest companies full stop.

The Indian Pacific pulls up alongside the Line of Lode that gave Broken Hill its reason for coming into being and by which it lives and dies.

The crowd on our coach is lively and pliable. There's a gasp on cue when we're told the miners' memorial above the station commemorates dead miners as young as 12. And there's polite laughter for the jokes.

"Over here is the Woolworths complex. If it burned to the ground, what would they call it? Coles."

"Down there is the Kevin Rudd building, otherwise known as the unemployment office."

It's anyone's guess how the then prime minister could be responsible for the consolidation and mechanisation that have reduced the need for miners.

The jokes at least fill some time because, truth be told, there isn't a lot to see in Broken Hill.

HOT SILVER

I don't know if the driver adapts his tour to a particular group but this morning the local nursing home gets a plug.

"There's an old house out the front of it and they were going to pull it down but a few people out of the South knew about it and they kicked up a bit of a stink and eventually they didn't. That's it over here on your left."

Further on we're introduced to *Law & Order: Broken Hill*.

"See the RSPCA here on our right? The police used to hide behind that and catch people speeding up and down here."

As tours go, not much of this worth putting in your travel journal.

The city is small. Within minutes we've seen all we're going to see of one side of Broken Hill — "We call it the north side" — and we're on our way to the other side — "We call it the south side".

Despite living in a city, and a tiny one at that, the citizens of Broken Hill are country people at heart and view the world as country people do, through the big end of the telescope. We pass the clubhouse of the Broken Hill Sea Scouts. It's an unexpected pastime for the youth of a dusty town five hours' drive from the ocean. Ah but, the driver says, the Menindee lakes are "just outside of town, about a hundred kilometres."

We see mostly mines and their admin buildings, which is hardly surprising. Everything connects to the mines, they're the heart of this ecosystem and they're decaying. The big tennis court was only open to mine workers and now isn't open at all. The mine the driver used to work for once had its own bowling club, pre-school and swimming pool. When the mines close, so does everything else and driving people round to look at what once was doesn't seem much of a replacement industry. There is some hope. A condemned power station has apparently caught the eye of a couple of production companies that would like to turn it into a film studio. Broken Hill isn't new to the movie business. *Mad Max* was filmed outside town; and the tour takes in the outside of the Palace Hotel, in which some of *Priscilla, Queen of the Desert* was filmed. The driver says he's pessimistic about a permanent studio opening in town, however. As I write this, Leonardo DiCaprio is in Sydney renting a $10,000-a-week waterfront mansion while shooting *The Great Gatsby*. It's hard to imagine him swapping that to be sipping midis at the Silver City Bowling Club while Gwyneth Paltrow takes a Zumba class in the hall.

Driving down the main street, Patton Street, we're told it was named for a mining engineer who came out in 1887 to help found the Zinc Corporation.

"Now I'm not 100 per cent sure on this, I have been told, and I think I've actually read it somewhere, but I have been told Bill was the father of General George Patton," says the bus driver.

I wonder what type of person might want to nail down this sort of fact. Tour guide perhaps? It certainly doesn't take more than a minute online to find out that General George S. Patton was a Jr, making his father a George Snr, not a Bill. But this was a tour with plenty of silences and the Great Patton Possibility fills a hole.

Something else I know is that Broken Hill is not a city that never sleeps. It's asleep right now and touring a place that's closed is odd. I know the streets are deserted and the shops locked up because everyone is still in bed but it makes the place lifeless and unappealing. It's not helped by the fact that the only progress we're learning about in Broken Hill is towards the Big Sleep.

"Broken Hill used to have well over 30 corner shops going back to the 1950s. Today we're down to about six," says the driver.

"This one here's still quite a successful little shop actually," he adds, allowing a touch of hope to creep in his voice.

Broken Hill would once have been one of the richest places in the world. In the 1950s the sea scouts could have

HOT SILVER

launched their dinghies in the only indoor heated swimming pool in New South Wales. Owned by the wealthy Zinc Corporation it attracted Olympians like Dawn Fraser to train in the months before the 1956 Melbourne games. Who knows, maybe even General Patton had a dip there, although that would have been terrifying for the sea scouts given that he was dead at the time.

A very much alive and freshly crowned Queen Elizabeth II certainly passed through Broken Hill in the 1950s, stopping for tea and scones supplied by the Zinc Corporation at their guest house.

"They tell me they smashed the toilet afterwards because they didn't want anyone in Broken Hill saying they sat on the same throne as Her Majesty had."

"They" have a lot to answer for this morning.

Our guide talks of the great, the good and the glory days when he can but many of his stories are of a more parochial nature, like the time one of his tour groups saw a boy kick his ball into a tree and the local firemen used their hose to knock it out. On the plus side, you won't get this sort of eye-witness reportage in the Lonely Planet entry for Broken Hill.

The tour of the closed shops of Broken Hill continues.

"About three doors down in the green and cream building you can see the butcher's. In the 1960s there was a butcher there, about six-foot-four, he had red hair and blue eyes. Guess what he weighed? Meat."

Groans this time. After an hour even our most tolerant travelling companions have found their limit.

No self-respecting bus tour doesn't disgorge its passengers into a shop where they can spend money and this one is no different. We're let off in sight of the train station but outside the Silver City Mint and Art Centre.

"It's about 20-to and we want youse back on the coach by about five past," the driver says.

We can't see anything else open but Fleur and I can see the train a block away and are hoping for at least for a café if we walk that way.

As the rest of the tour files into the "mint", Fleur and I thank the driver and say we'll be walking to the train from here.

"Are you sure you don't want to go in?" he asks. "The painting is quite something."

We'd been told as we approached the mint that there was within — "just through the opal cave" — the world's biggest painting by a single artist. Size is generally a reliable indication of artistic merit when it's given such prominence in the advertising. It indicates that the work is shit. Do you know the dimensions of the Mona Lisa or the circumference of The Thinker's bicep? Would da Vinci or Rodin have considered it a career highlight to make it into *Ripley's Believe It or Not*? I know my answers but I can't look the driver in the eye and tell him we have no interest in one of the few treasures Broken Hill has managed to hang onto. So it is we find ourselves walking through a souvenir shop into a papier-mâché "opal cave" and onto the walkway from which we are to admire an enormous canvas panorama of the outback. The wooden walkway is done to look like the veranda of an outback station, complete with a sloping wooden roof above. To complete the effect, the floor between the edge of the walkway and the canvas is strewn with rocks, plastic shrubs and at least a metric tonne of red dirt. Unseen floodlights shine uniformly on the canvas. If I kidnapped you and ripped off your blindfold in this spot, you would later swear to police that you'd been held on the soundstage of *The Three Amigos*.

"Many artists," the blurb says, "can be paralysed by that moment when they stare at a blank canvas. Imagine the overwhelming feeling of facing a blank canvas measuring almost 100 metres long and 12 metres at its highest point!"

If only the artist had been paralysed by the size of the

task in hand; then Fleur and I might have had more time to look for the coffee we so badly need. As it is we are now paralysed ourselves by the enormity of what we're looking at. It is truly awful. The painting is as kitsch as a Jesus snow globe and bigger and more monstrous than you can imagine. Such is the creative force of the genius behind this artwork that he named it… drumroll, please… "The Big Picture". The artist himself goes by the diminutive name "Ando", which makes him sound more like a children's magician than an artist.

He is also responsible for Mundi Man, an "Andoscope" carved into over four million square metres of the Mundi Mundi Plains in New South Wales. It's a head and shoulders cartoon of a stockman whose smile "is as wide as the Empire State Building is tall!"

"Ando likes to work in a big format," his website says redundantly.

"I have done hundreds of paintings of landscapes on canvas but this is the first time I have used the landscape as my canvas!" writes Ando on the site, where he paints as good a self-portrait with his frequent exclamation marks as he might with his brushes.

The piece is six times larger than what was previously the world's largest artwork. That one was made when 11 Florida islands were wrapped by Christo, another delusionist who can't distinguish between the size of an artwork and the talent of its artist. It's only a matter of time before Ando and Christo are in hot competition to cast the World's Heaviest Statue.

The Amazing Ando, a son of Broken Hill, is summed up well in the description of The Big Picture on the Mint's website as "an incredible feat for an artist who has never had an art lesson in his life! A picture may say a thousand words, but Ando's paintings will leave you speechless!"

Speechless indeed, we walk out to find Strepsils in a newsagent and grab a coffee in a café close to the train.

Although we had our own compartment and quickly took to keeping the door shut, you're never truly alone on the Indian Pacific. This is not a holiday in which you're in control. As soon as you start to relax there's a reminder that you're marching to the beat of someone else's timetable. There are constant announcements about meals piped into the compartments. Two sittings three times a day means two announcements that dinner will be served shortly; two announcements that it's being served; and two announcements that someone's going to miss the gravy boat if he doesn't hustle to the dining car. There are announcements about time zone changes, tours and what's outside the window. Once the PA in our compartment suddenly and without explanation came alive with a medley of ballads about Irish outlaws. It was like the soundtrack for a train robbery. I wouldn't have been surprised to look out of the window to see half a dozen masked men on horseback firing six shooters over their heads.

Where I had imagined us sitting back in our compartment, reading then wandering up to the bar car for a coffee and a browse through some magazines, that's not the way it works. It's up at dawn for Broken Hill; back on the train for an hour or so of breakfast; back to the compartment for a short break; then a long lunch. By the time we got to Adelaide at the end of the second day, it felt like we'd been constantly on the go.

· Adelaide ·

The train pulls into Adelaide on schedule just after 3 p.m. My old boss Liz is waiting on the platform like an angel of mercy whose local knowledge (and car) we need for a fast scavenger hunt. I have three hours to get to a pub, drink much beer, and visit a pharmacy and a supermarket to stock up for the days ahead. I can't face the dining car without Fleur. We're three meals into the trip and even with two of us rubbing verbal sticks together we've yet to spark a real conversation with the strangers who've lost at musical chairs and had to sit with us. There's been buzz and ho-ho through the rest of the Queen Adelaide dining car — "I hope the driver's charged the batteries in his GPS!" Dining with us, however, is clearly a chore. I'd hoped we might pay our way with telegraphs from the 21st century — "We use this thing called Facebook" — but my hopes have evaporated as completely as the moisture in the air on the train.

The average age of the disembarking passengers had not been lost on Liz as she waited for us on the platform. Our eyes meet as we walk towards her. The twinkle in hers tells me she's guessed this trip has not been what I was expecting. The bulging in mine tells her she was right. This wordless exchange suffices until we are safely in the car. Like bank robbers commandeering a getaway vehicle, we basically order her to drive, drive, drive. As we swing out of the station car park, we prioritise food and medical supplies so the first stop is a strip mall, where I grab armfuls of Strepsils and a palette-load of tissues. Then Fleur and I hit the supermarket.

I have some experience with catering a train journey for one. My schoolboy trip through China and Eastern Europe happened when the Berlin Wall was still standing and the iron rice bowl was close to empty. We took extra food but were limited to what we could carry and what would last for up to six weeks. These considerations had escaped one teacher whose Danish houseguest had baked her 15 family-sized apple strudels for the trip. After a week or so, probably when she realised her unrefrigerated desserts were on the turn, Strudel (we gave out imaginative nicknames) brought a tray to our compartment. We thanked her, closed the door, pulled down the window and threw the strudel from a moving train into a Chinese field, shouting "Enjoy this, peasants!" Say what you like about capitalists, our teenagers are the envy of the world.

My supplies for travel behind the Iron Curtain comprised half a dozen packets of Ryvita and jars of peanut butter, Marmite and jam. Often the dining cars had no supplies and our personal stores provided the only meals we had. My diary from this trip, arguably my first piece of travel writing, includes entries like:

"Dinner: Cheez Balls, Tang, cocoa."

"Breakfast: Finished Cheez Balls. Tea, tomato soup and peanuts."

"Lunch: 5 Ryvita — peanut butter, pâté (from Richard) and marmalade. Tea, 5 ginger nuts, 4 little melons."

"Dinner: Vitamin pill."

The fact that one of my 16-year-old companions was travelling with pâté says as much about us as our hilarious strudel-throwing japes.

What my menus lacked in potential for a spin-off cookery series, they made up for in weight loss. By the end of the trip I couldn't buckle my bum bag tightly enough to stop it falling down over my (even then unfashionable) stonewash jeans. I had to tie the strap in a knot to keep it from falling off.

Two decades later and with the bounty of a Foodland supermarket all around me, I find out that in a crisis my palate regresses to that of a teenage boy. We race down the aisles with me grabbing at packets of Shapes, Vegemite scrolls, quiches, bags of crisps and a selection of fun-size candy bars. To look at the carb content in my shopping basket you would think I was fuelling myself to push the train not ride in it.

For Fleur this was her last stop, her e-ticket on a flight to Sydney as golden to her at this point as Charlie Bucket's ticket to the chocolate factory. In the pub she and Liz worked hard to persuade me to abandon the train and fly back to Sydney, too. I was tempted but couldn't. I was on the train to make a travel feature and felt journalistic integrity required me to see the trip through to the end. I can't tell you how often it is that we travel journalists are left to teach ethics to the others. At the heart of my decision there was also a bloody-minded refusal to let the Indian Pacific beat me, even if its passengers had forced me to retreat to my compartment and eat supermarket quiche. Mostly, however, I wanted to see the Nullarbor Plain. I wanted to have crossed Australia by train, even if it did suck a bit.

Liz drove us back through a bleak industrial estate to Adelaide Parklands Terminal, which is to Sydney's Central Station as Costco is to the Harrods Food Hall.

One word from me and Liz would have made a handbrake turn and taken us both to the airport but I couldn't be swayed. When I hugged Fleur she looked genuinely worried about me. I had to remind myself this was supposedly a luxury journey; and I'd be remiss if I didn't say that did indeed seem to be what my fellow passengers were enjoying.

Fleur and Liz drove off and I took the long walk down the platform to stock my larder. Except I couldn't. It was about 6 p.m. and the train didn't leave for another 40 minutes so it was locked.

I felt conspicuous walking back to the terminal with my bags of shopping swinging against my legs but it was too cold to stand on the platform. I certainly didn't need anything from the terminal café, Choo Choos, so I made myself as comfortable as possible in a plastic chair and waited for the tube to be unlocked.

STEVEN LEWIS

On the second night of my Indian Pacific adventure I dine alone on quiche watching *Treme* on the MacBook Pro.

The sights of Broken Hill

Recovering from the Big Picture

A curious bystander on the platform at Broken Hill

Writing on the train

HOT SILVER

Braving the dining car

My compartment seen from the platform in Adelaide

Day Three
ALONE ON THE PLAIN

· Compartment 11/12 ·

Penny, today's hospitality assistant, surprises me by bringing my 6.30 a.m. cup of tea at six. Fortunately I'm awake if bleary-eyed but there's a delay while I throw on some trousers. I can see Penny is surprised that any of her charges might still be in his bunk at this late hour. I think of the early-risers making a pre-dawn raid on the muffins yesterday and of my mother, who is usually making lunch by this time of the morning.

I take a shower and turn off the lights in the compartment so I can watch the dawn catch the train. I'm facing backwards so I can see it chasing us, slowly at first. The rising sun is just strong enough to silhouette some wispy trees against the grey sky. A stronger copper light begins to split the sky into an area of dark blue and another, lighter blue edged with white. Eventually that white edge mixes through the blue until the sun has completed its work and the whole sky is a uniform limpid blue. It clashes brightly with the red earth and the dull green shrubs covering it.

My notebook from this point is punctuated with these poetic descriptions of the world outside my window. The train is travelling at a constant speed but I can see I'm slowing down, taking it in, appreciating more. Mobile reception can be patchy even in urban Australia. Out here you're more likely to see wild unicorns than get a mobile signal, let alone the internet. I will be out of touch with the world until we pull into Kalgoorlie after dark.

This is the first day I can see myself channelling my inner Paul Theroux. The journey has not been restful so far. Today it's up at 6 a.m. — thank you for the dawn, Penny — breakfast at 7 a.m. then a half hour stop at 8 a.m. followed by nothing before Kalgoorlie at 7.10 p.m. I plan to spend the time barricaded in my compartment, reading, writing and watching some more of the hours of TV I loaded onto my Mac before we left.

At some point we'll be stopping briefly to make a mail drop at Watson, a siding south of Maralinga. The PA system tells us breezily that Maralinga is where the British and Australian governments tested nuclear bombs in the 1950s and 1960s. Later I look it up. The first major set of tests in 1956, Operation Buffalo, involved detonating four bombs with gentle codenames like Marcoo and Kite. Where the regular military likes to get to the point with names like Hellfire, Stinger and Trident, it seems their nuclear cousins need to distance themselves from the aims of their work.

One Tree, a bomb roughly equivalent in power to Little Boy, produced a mushroom cloud that reached 37,500 feet over Maralinga and fallout was detected in almost every Australian state and territory. Afterwards servicemen were ordered to run, walk and crawl across ground contaminated by the fallout. A 1999 study found that 30 per cent of them had since died from cancer, mostly in their fifties.

The clean up of the site, which didn't start until the late 1990s, cost the Australian and British governments over $100 million. The Australian government also paid the local aboriginal people compensation of $14 million, but not until 1994 and after a number of them had gone blind or developed cancers.

It seems trivial that the government that poisoned their land has nonetheless kept up delivery of the mail.

The window of a train is a rolling series of vignettes. From time to time between Sydney and Adelaide Fleur and I would catch glimpses of lives being lived; a house, a farm building, a grain silo, lambs in a paddock, a ute parked on a hill. We would wonder about the unseen people they belonged to. After Adelaide there are fewer traces of habitation. There are, however, a number of small towns like Gladstone.

HOT SILVER

Gladstone, population 629, is one of the last handful of towns the Indian Pacific passes through before reaching the Nullarbor Plain. From my window I see a slack-jawed boy of about 12 watching us go by from a camping chair on the back porch of his house. According to Wikipedia the town has "two pubs, three churches, a bank, a Post Office and several shops and small businesses providing basic goods and services". The local school has 205 students "drawn from the wider district". There would have been that many students in a single year group at my school. As a 12-year-old my idea of "basic goods and services" came from vast air-conditioned shopping malls populated by thousands of shoppers and Hong Kong's first multiplex cinemas. What did this boy do, I wondered, in the hours between trains passing?

Later on the Nullarbor Plain we'll motor past a modest area of solar panels badged with a Lions Club logo. I'll want to know what they power. Who lives out here? Other people's lives are little mysteries when you glimpse them for seconds from a window. If the world's stock markets lost 10,000 points in overnight trading, what impact would it have out here?

After Port Augusta there's even less to wonder about.

The Nullarbor Plain

"Nullarbor" is said to come from the Latin "nullus", meaning "no", and "arbor", meaning "tree". That's open to dispute. What isn't, however, is that it is truly as if the person running nature's tree-seeding machine abruptly turned around for home once he reached the edge of this plain. One minute there are trees flying past the window of the train and the next minute there are not. Everything drops away to a flat, monotonous nothingness. There is an absence all the way to the horizon in every direction. Sure, there is red-brown dirt and a plentiful helping of shrubs the size of decent rocks; but like a smile with a missing tooth, it's what you don't see that absorbs you. From the train window to the edge of the world there is nothing between earth and sky. The negative space is eerie, as if the world has disappeared.

At its widest point, the Plain is 1,100 kilometres, roughly the distance between New York and Chicago. It has an area of 200,000 square kilometres, which is about the same as England and Scotland combined. Those two countries are between them home to around 58 million people. The population of the Nullarbor Plain could meet in the tray of a ute and still pick up hitchhikers.

Edward John Eyre, a Bedfordshire man who became the first European to cross the Plain, described it as "a hideous anomaly, a blot on the face of Nature, the sort of place one gets into in bad dreams". I couldn't have disagreed with him more. In desperation I had taken to leaving a cup of water on a little shelf in the compartment, hoping to return some humidity to the air. I was also chain-sucking Strepsils and using every corner of my tissues for fear of running out and having to sand my nose on the locked supply of toilet paper. Nonetheless the view from my window was worth the price of admission. There might have been nothing to see but it was a privilege to be seeing it.

In fairness to Eyre, his journey across the Nullarbor in 1840 was marginally more uncomfortable than mine. For a start he was on foot, not in a train compartment with an en suite bathroom. His expedition failed at first when three of his horses died of dehydration. He set out again with fellow explorer John Baxter, three aboriginal men, and still not enough water. When that became an issue, two of the aboriginal men murdered Baxter with a shotgun and stole the remaining supplies. Eyre had no choice but to leave Baxter's remains wrapped in a shroud and press on with the remaining aboriginal man. They eventually made it, eating whatever they could find along the way, including pelican, several of their horses, and at least one wedge-tailed eagle. The journey had taken eight months.

I figure he was entitled to consider the Nullarbor Plain a bitch.

The Trans-Australian Railway line, which we're on now, means we can make the Nullarbor crossing in a day, including riding the longest straight section of track in the world. Enough of it, at 478 kilometres, to make a Roman weep with envy. It's certainly a bloody long way to travel in a straight line, equivalent — for those of you enjoying the distance comparisons — to the rail journey between London and Paris.

The line was started in 1917 by teams leaving simultaneously from Kalgoorlie in Western Australia and Port Augusta in South Australia. They met in the centre at Ooldea within the year. The harsh weather played havoc with the railway as the track flexed in the desert sands, making for slow and difficult journeys. The whole line was rebuilt in 1969 in time for the Indian Pacific to roll across it for the first time in 1970 with its full water tanks and a menu that didn't require a taste for penguin, horse or eagle.

HOT SILVER

The wedge-tailed eagle, incidentally, was not chosen as the Indian Pacific's totem just because Australians are second only to American Indians in attaching animals to human activities. Qantas, the airline that still calls Australia home despite an increasingly expatriate base of operations, is known as the "flying kangaroo". In Australian sport native sea eagles, wallabies and sharks play exotics like lions, swans and bulldogs.

The eagle was actually chosen because it's Australia's largest bird of prey, big enough to kill an adult kangaroo. Its massive wingspan — up to 2.3 metres — symbolises the breadth of the Indian Pacific's journey across the country.

It probably helped the wedge-tailed eagle's chances of getting the gig with Great Southern Rail that it has been known to attack planes and helicopters. This uncompromising approach to the tube's competitors no doubt further endeared the angry eagle to the last of the great Australian railwaymen.

It's appropriate that the Nullarbor Plain is the place on the trip where the eagle is most likely to be seen gliding on its enormous wings. Even though we'd been on the Indian Pacific for a day and a half by the time we hit the Nullarbor, nowhere is the scale of the endeavour more apparent than on this leg.

· Cook ·

We break our journey across the Nullarbor several times, pausing for the driver to drop off and pick up post at the side of the track. Whom the mail is for, God only knows. I imagine a group of Star Wars Sand People emerging from cover after we pass and ripping into their boxes from Amazon. Rurrgh, rargh Kindle? Eyurgha, rugha *30 Rock* season one!

We passengers don't get off the train during these pauses. For us there is one stop on the Nullarbor Plain, the township of Cook. The rich baritone piped into our compartments tells us that Cook once had a population of 40 souls, making it a "bustling town". Where I'm from 40 people wouldn't be considered a bus queue. Today I judge a place by its proximity to an Apple store. Being within walking distance of an Apple store proper puts you at the centre of modern civilisation. Concentric rings work out from there until you get to the outer ring, which is where there are no Apple stores but you're still within driving distance of a specialist Mac retailer. Outside that it's *Game of Thrones* territory; you're beyond the Wall. Cook is five hours' drive from anywhere and even then you'd just be pausing to refuel your four-wheel drive. It'd be another 12 hours before you were anywhere you'd be able to buy an iPad and read the *Vanity Fair* app over a latte. In my dictionary Cook defines the middle of nowhere.

Implanted in the dust of the Nullarbor in 1917, Cook's purpose was to service the trains passing through. In its day it must have been quite a place. Not only were there houses for the workers but there was a hospital; a golf course; a school for the children; and a swimming pool where the kids could strip off and count who had the most toes. The inbreeding alone must have kept the hospital busy. They would have needed the pool, too; temperatures out here can reach the high 40s (nearly 120 degrees

Fahrenheit).

The facilities sound lavish for a handful of railway workers and their families, the fruits of working in a nationalised industry. When the railways were privatised in 1997 the lifeguard called the children out of the pool for the last time; the sick were tipped from their hospital beds; and tee times at the Cook Golf Course were rudely cancelled. Under capitalism Cook was demoted to nothing more than pumping diesel and water into the trains. It's a role that requires no more than the current population of five.

When Cook comes into view I ask myself who on earth these five desperadoes might be. From the look of the place they must be on the run from the law or atoning for their part in some off-the-books massacre in a southeast Asian jungle. Nothing else would possess me to live all the way out here, especially not in the conditions I can see from my window.

The train stops opposite a huddle of huts standing shoulder to shoulder against the elements. It's 17 degrees outside and the wind is strong enough to launch Richard Branson into orbit from a standing start. There is no platform, the train just stops and we jump off. It's like we're on a road trip and Dad's pulled onto the hard shoulder for us to take in a view or stretch our legs and find a tree to pee behind. Except we're not in a car, we're in over half a kilometre of train and there's not a lot to see. There is, however, plenty to pee behind.

I emerge from the train with the cast of *Cocoon* and we pick our way across the hard brown ground, fleeces pulled tight against the wind. There is no "tour" of Cook and no instruction that anything is off limits. I wouldn't like to trespass into the houses occupied by the remaining five custodians but it's impossible to pick out which ones are abandoned and which are in use. All the buildings look as derelict as the small groups now inspecting them. "Gardens" are fenced off with aluminium sheeting but panels have blown off and are scattered around. None of the huts has a flowering window box, a welcome mat and a copy of the *Cook Gazette* lying on the path.

Behind the first row of huts is a shed with no windows. Its wide awning shades a row of mismatched office chairs and a single stuffed armchair that looks as if an inch has been taken off one of its legs. Also under cover is a giant cable spool turned on its side. Could it be used as a bar table to stand around at the end of the working day? There are enough chairs on the dusty veranda for the whole population of Cook to sit and watch the world go by, except it won't.

What I speculate is a social club could just as easily be the place where the people of Cook dump their unwanted chairs. Either way, these are signs of habitation, of people, yet there are no people to be seen. It's like walking round one of those fake towns the Americans tested their nuclear weapons on. I wouldn't be surprised to turn a corner and find mannequin Betty Draper holding a plastic cigarette to her bright cherry lips waiting for the bomb to drop. And if the Reds didn't blow her to kingdom come, the wind just might.

Behind one building two utes are parked nose to tail and going nowhere. They're rusted into place, one with no tyres and the other with flat ones. Is this what happens in Cook? When you've finished with something, a car, a chair, you just walk away from it and leave it to rust or decay. There is, after all, no shortage of space out here. The view from the front window of every house is the Nullarbor Plain stretching to the horizon, flat, brown and scrubby. The view will be familiar to the occupants of the front room because it's the same one they saw from their bedroom when they woke up; from the kitchen when they had breakfast; and from every other window in the house. What the place lacks in visual relief it makes up for in thousands of square kilometres in which to abandon your crap.

It's not surprising to find the residents take their relief in a wit as dry as the relentless wind. A hand-painted sign labels 20 metres of potholed Astroturf as the "Cook Cricket Club". It's a one-trick wit, though. The chicken wire fence around a weathered multisport surface has a sign in the same hand — the "Cook Country Club". A fondness for repetition is probably a necessary trait among those who've chosen to live in a unvaried landscape to do jobs dictated by a railway timetable.

The clubhouse is a shed whose paint has mostly blistered off, leaving the steel exposed. For refreshments there's a white kitchen fridge lying on its back between the clubhouse and the tennis net flapping in the breeze. The surface rust gives it a crème brûlée effect.

Cook is a desolate place and I've seen enough of it when the wail of an air-raid siren tells us it's time to get back on the train before the next H-bomb goes off. We've been warned there is no headcount to check against and I don't want to be left behind so I hurry back.

After Cook the train manager pipes a bizarre mix tape into our compartments. Mike and the Mechanics step aside for a thigh-slapping banjo trio singing about swagmen before we're put in the hands of Paul McCartney and Stevie Wonder. I never get the hang of the in-compartment radio. There is no discernible reason why it's on or off. If it's a good thing to deliver 80s pop and bush poetry to our compartments sometimes, why not all the time? Who at Great Southern Rail rolled out a map of the journey on the boardroom table and decided which landscapes to score and which to snub with silence? And while I certainly understood the bush ballads, what was it about the Nullarbor Plain that suggested *Ebony and Ivory*?

The musical smorgasbord is seasoned with short lectures on kangaroos and other topics relevant to what's outside the windows. These are genuinely fascinating, particularly the explanation that this expanse of nothingness was made possible only because this empty place was once completely the opposite. The ocean was here, teeming with the billions of sea creatures whose bodies became the Nullarbor Plain, the world's largest limestone surface.

Perhaps it was the desolation of Cook that made me decide to try the dining car for the first time since Adelaide. I take a seat in a booth with Mary, her middle-aged daughter Caroline, and Doreen, an elderly widow from Queensland.

The food is excellent, as it has been every time I've been in the Queen Adelaide dining car. This time it's a main course of pie with sticky banana pudding for "afters" but I'm out of my depth in the conversation. When they're talking about dementia — Mary and Doreen both lost husbands to it — I don't know how to arrange my face or what to say. I feel callow. I'm no better off when the talk shifts to lighter matters. I have nothing to contribute when Doreen talks about how hard it is to find a butcher who stocks kangaroo tail. If I am lucky enough to find a butcher in Mosman who keeps it, Doreen tells me, the best way to cook it is in foil in the oven. It seems the polite thing to do so I make a note in my book.

I mention that I'm disappointed there wasn't a shop in Cook. I would have spent money on anything just to have something new to look at.

Oh there was a shop, say the ladies. Didn't I see it? No, I bloody well didn't. I would have killed for a bar of chocolate. Anything. I might even have bought a kangaroo scrotum coin purse — where there are souvenirs in Australia, there is always a kangaroo scrotum coin purse. I might have mounted it on a stick in my compartment, called it Wilson and talked to it all the way to Perth.

This is how I learn that Cook's five residents run a shop that opens just a few times a week and for only half an hour each time. Some might think this tight window for commerce would dictate aggressive marketing — an announcement over the PA before arrival, banners at intervals the length of the train… Then again, the members of the Cook Chamber of Commerce aren't in Cook for their love of crowds. The ladies had stumbled on a small sign advertising the shop's presence. Looking on Flickr at someone else's pictures of Cook, I see the sign now. It's one of those witty directions signs; "Perth", it says, pointing one way down the track; "Sydney", the other. Underneath Sydney it says "Souvenirs". The sign is as plain as day as long as you happen to get out of the car that is next to it. If you've been travelling in one of the other 22 cars along over 600 metres of train, tough luck, fella.

I picture the shopkeepers retiring to the Cable Spool Social Club after the rush and reminiscing about when they were nationalized and on hot days didn't bother to get out of the pool to open the shop at all.

Mary, Caroline and Doreen have an easy rapport at lunch that I try to fake but it's tiring. I am an impostor and go back to my compartment to wait for Kalgoorlie.

· Kalgoorlie ·

I'm looking forward to Kalgoorlie, really for no other reason that it's synonymous with the outback and the outback is a profound part of the spirit of my adopted country. Almost all Australians live along the coast, venturing inland only as far as is necessary to find a collection of vineyards with cellar doors. Nonetheless there is a part of every Australian that sees himself pulling out crocodile teeth to decorate his hatband.

The town's name comes from an aboriginal word meaning "place of the silky pears" but the value of Kalgoorlie comes not from its appeal to greengrocers but from the massive deposits of gold, nickel and other minerals in the region. With its concentration of mines this "Golden Mile" is possibly the richest square mile on the planet. Yet the town might never have come to be if a horse hadn't cast a shoe in the area in 1893, causing three Irish prospectors to stop long enough to look around and notice signs of gold. Was there ever a luckier horse shoe?

The Indian Pacific pulls into Kalgoorlie at 7.10 on a Monday night so naturally it's shut. This is a theme of the Indian Pacific. Broken Hill was in bed. Adelaide is not a lively place at the best of times and we arrived mid-afternoon on a Sunday, two hours before the law requires shops to shut to prevent South Australians being overwhelmed by having too much to do. Cook of course is permanently shut.

There is a "whistle stop" tour of Kalgoorlie offered but by this stage I feel I've toured more than enough closed towns to satisfy journalistic integrity.

A blogger on the aptly-named "Why Go?" site writes that it was much debated on her Indian Pacific journey whether a night tour of Kalgoorlie would be worth it. She was prompted to take the tour precisely to answer this perfectly sensible question. Kalgoorlie is hardly Las Vegas, after all, and its lack of bright lights is exactly the problem. There are, she notes, few street lights in the mining town. In the gloom apparently you could still make out from the bus the "shape and design" of the buildings that were being talked about by the guide. Sounds brilliant.

"What did you make of Kalgoorlie?"

"Lovely shapes."

The tour does also take in a giant open cast mine — the Super Pit, created by Alan Bond. As a 24-hour operation, at least it's floodlit and it would be an interesting sight. The hole is so huge that when the mine is closed in 2017 it's expected to take 50 years to fill with groundwater.

The tour wraps up with a drive-past of Kalgoorlie's once-thriving red-light district, now reduced to three brothels. My marriage contract obliges me to say here that I'm not an expert on brothels but I'm told their most appealing shapes are *inside* the building. It seems unlikely, therefore, that much justice is done to their attractions from the window of a passing coach. Apparently one of them is also a museum of the oldest profession. Were the train stopping longer, I could have entered on the excuse of going in to "see the exhibits".

My interests at this point lie in neither opencast nor open legs but in food that doesn't come in a foil wrapper or, if it does, someone is going to open it for me and put it in a microwave. I follow some groups of passengers walking down Wilson Street away from the train station. On the corner I spot the last open shop in town, which is, thank the unhealthy gods of mining, a pharmacy. By the time I've stocked up on tissues and a selection of throat lozenges, I'm on my own again.

I take a left turn onto Hannan Street, which seems to be the main drag. From what I can see Kalgoorlie is a great-looking country town, so close to how I would imagine one that it could have been commissioned by a film studio. The pavement is sheltered by the joined porticos of single-storey shops. Decorative Dutch gables of every shape raise the shops from boxes to something with a simple, orderly elegance. You can't tell much about a city by walking down main street after dark on a Monday night. All I can say is that it looks like a neat, tidy and plain-speaking sort of place.

Two aboriginal men stop and introduce themselves to me as the traditional owners of the town. They ask me if I have any money and if they could have my hat. They are unsteady on their feet but friendly. I give them a little rent but walk on when they ask a second time for my hat.

There are cities in which you would be spoiled for choice in restaurants even on a Monday evening but Kalgoorlie isn't one of them. A little way down the street, I spot somewhere that looks open and walk towards it. What I'd seen was the two-storey Exchange Hotel, which dominates the corner of Maritana and Hannan Streets. Its rust-coloured dormer roof and wraparound first-floor veranda command each of the two streets and its cupola is the focal point of the intersection of the two.

On the ground floor is Paddy's Ale House Irish Pub, presumably named for Patrick "Paddy" Hannan, he of the street name and one of the Irish prospectors whose careless horse discovered the Kalgoorlie goldfield. There is seating under a portico supported on pairs of green wrought iron pillars. After 12 hours in our airless tube, I don't care how cold it is, I'm sitting outside.

In contrast to the functional name of the Exchange Hotel in which it sits, "Paddy's Ale House Irish Pub" seems less a name than a collection of keywords strung together for search engine optimisation. It's described paradoxically on one website as an "authentic" Irish theme pub. Inside it is indeed a fine example of the Irish kit pub genre — there's beer, giant TVs, and dark furniture that's lighter to pick up than you would think by looking at it. The dominance of dusty boots and work shirts with fluorescent strips mark this out as a pub for locals as well as soft blow-ins like me.

I order a chicken burger and wait for it outside. It's a cool night but it's a pleasure to be in the fresh air.

I call Fleur, eat my burger, read my book then head for the train. I have half an hour to make a 10 minute walk but I'm still terrified of being left behind.

The Nullarbor Plain

Cook seen from the train

Fleece patrol

Abandoned home?

HOT SILVER

Cable Spool Social Club

Cook Municipal Car Park

63

Cook Country Club

Behind the clubhouse

Day Four
HOME TIME

· Perth ·

I wake up to find someone has turned the trees back on. An early morning fog hangs over lush farmland that we fly past. The farms are exactly as I, the city boy, think of farms — neat fences, trim outbuildings, groomed earth and the occasional picturesque piece of rusting machinery. I have husbanded my Adelaide stores well and still have a muesli bar left for breakfast so for the last time I ignore the announcement for my meal sitting.

The outskirts of Perth are a relief, bringing with them internet access and a chance to call Fleur. I wish I could say that my frustration and gripes with the Indian Pacific had dissolved with the rocking of the train but they hadn't. As we approach Perth, I feel exactly as anyone would who had been sick for a couple of days and spent most of them locked in a compartment on an airless train.

My trip comes to an end when the train pulls into East Perth station at 9.10 on a Tuesday morning. I had booked my flight from Perth to Sydney to allow me some time to see Perth where I had never been but I've had enough of places I've never been, even if this was the first time we were arriving in one that would actually be open to receive us. I want to get back to Sydney as soon as possible. And, via a taxi from the station to the airport, that's exactly what I do.

Epilogue
A RAILWAYMANS HOLIDAY

"We deliver people's dreams, their dreams to see the country."
Tony Braxton-Smith
CEO, Great Southern Rail

In September 2011 the chief executive of Great Southern Rail, Tony Braxton-Smith, kicked off the second season of the Australian version of *Undercover Boss*. In this reality TV show a CEO goes "undercover" in his own organisation, coming down from the mountain to work with a selection of the lowest level employees to find out what life is like at the bottom of the pile. According to the introductory voiceover the show is about CEOs who "dare to be different" and "take extreme action". Their first extreme action is usually growing an extremely scruffy beard because we all know that's what the working classes look like, even the women. "Extreme times," we're told "call for extreme measures." And beards.

The staff he encounters are told a film crew is making a documentary about someone who wants to change profession. In this case they were asked to swallow the idea that "Sidney King" — "Sid" to the working man — was looking for a career change from accountant to train cleaner, kitchen hand, hospitality assistant or baggage handler. The CEO "swaps his corporate suit for a flouro vest" in four locations, one for each of the jobs he tries. He's paired in each place with one or two employees who show him how to do their jobs. The workers are carefully chosen by the production team to be not just Stakhanovites but ones with heart-warming backstories. In this case, among others, he works with a young hospitality assistant whose father died not long ago; and a Vietnamese chef who escaped his homeland after being imprisoned by the North Vietnamese.

As part of his Damascene journey Braxton-Smith travelled on the Indian Pacific, which is how I learned that the stewards are in fact hospitality assistants or HAs. I also learned that the cleaning of the toilets is known as "doing the silvers"; and I was reminded that blocked silvers are such a problem that there's a light next to each toilet that flashes angry red if you've overloaded the bowl.

Working as a hospitality assistant in the dining car, "Sid" has trouble coming to grips with the four-box grid system on the ordering pad. It's a complex system in which each box represents a person in the booth. Four persons, four boxes. Stay with me. It's made curlier by having to remember that each box has to be marked "T for tart" or "S for sausages", a code derived from the fact that the main course choice this lunch service is between tart and sausages. It's a lot to take in so the young hospitality assistant explains this slowly to Tony, whose jaw is hanging loose with his confusion.

"It's like a crossword," he says. "There's a risk I'll give someone the wrong meal."

"Sid" is duly shown carrying four meals from the galley to a booth containing only one passenger. Thank God he's not responsible for distributing their meds.

"To me it seems that there could be a simple change to that form that could make it a little more foolproof," says Tony, who knows his fools. No doubt staff can expect a flash flood of profound changes to flow from head office as a result of Tony's undercover investigation.

The staff shown were mostly as I remembered them: young, decent, pleasant, and working in cramped conditions for passengers old enough to be their grandparents.

At the end of each episode the employees who've been paired with the undercover boss are summoned to head office. It's part of the entertainment that the CEO toys with them by not telling them why they've been summoned. They are filmed in the back of taxis visibly nervous they're about to be fired. What fun the viewers have when the CEO — now restored to management good looks by a quick shave in the office sink — enters a meeting room to reveal his true identity and bestow his largesse on a relieved underling. That there will be a reward is

HOT SILVER

mandated by the format of the show, which is why featured employees have to be screened beforehand for worthiness. It's also why they must have a touching backstory. This allows the boss to show off more of his awesome power by magicing away some of the pain of their personal lives as well as giving a work-related treat.

The cleaning lady is given a trip to New Zealand to see her sons and the opportunity to host a "cleaning summit" in Alice Springs. There she will teach other cleaners her system of matching blue chemicals to blue cloths and green chemicals to green cloths. In his half hour of doing the silvers Tony had struggled with this colour-coding as much as he had with the order pad.

The Vietnamese chef is given a trip to Vietnam with his wife — but not his four children — to see his 86-year-old mother whom he is not paid enough otherwise to see more than once every five years.

The best reward the CEO can conceive is saved for the baggage handler and the young hospitality assistants. No overseas holidays and order-pad summits for them. They are given first class passage on the trains on which they work every day.

I imagine them on their railwayman's holiday, squeezed into a booth in the dining car, and wish them well.

ACKNOWLEDGEMENTS

The author travelled on the Indian Pacific courtesy of Great Southern Rail for a travel feature that appeared in the inflight entertainment of V Australia. That feature is now available on Audible.

Many of the photographs in this book – certainly the better ones – were taken by Fleur Lewis.

ABOUT THE AUTHOR

A journalist and writer for nearly 20 years, Steven Lewis has written for the *Financial Times*, *Esquire*, *GQ*, the *International Herald Tribune* and other publications around the world. A long-time resident of Hong Kong, he had popular television and consumer technology columns in the *South China Morning Post*. He was also the technology editor of *Asian Business*. His audio travel programs are part of the inflight entertainment on several airlines.

He first published online in 1994 and today his titles are in print, electronic and audio versions from Amazon, Apple and Audible, among others.

Steven is also a professional podcaster and ghostwriter. He helps other writers publish their ebooks through his blog at Taleist (www.taleist.com).

Steven lives in Sydney with his wife and son, Jack.

CPSIA information can be obtained
at www.ICGtesting.com
Printed in the USA
BVHW03s2107270618
520208BV00001B/64/P